Calm Wealth

Mastering Money in an Anxious World

Ed Merid

"This book will help you make clear, confident financial decisions without anxiety, even when the future feels uncertain."

Table of Contents

AUTHOR'S NOTE 5

Introduction 7

Chapter 1: Why Money Feels So Heavy 10

Chapter 2: The Mind Under Financial Pressure 18

Chapter 3: Your Personal Money Triggers 27

Chapter 4: From Fear to Clarity 35

Chapter 5: Staying Calm When Money Feels Urgent 43

Chapter 6: Designing a Calm Wealth System 52

Chapter 7: Making Decisions in an Uncertain World 61

Chapter 8: Calm Wealth for Life 70

Conclusion: Choosing Calm, Again and Again 78

AUTHOR'S NOTE

This book was not written to teach you how to beat the market, optimize every dollar, or eliminate financial uncertainty from your life.

It was written because I noticed something quieter, and far more common.

I met intelligent, responsible people who were doing "everything right" with money, yet felt constantly tense. People who planned carefully, earned reasonably well, and avoided reckless behavior, but still carried a persistent sense of financial unease. Not panic. Not crisis. Just a steady background pressure that never seemed to turn off.

What struck me was that their stress rarely came from numbers alone. It came from responsibility, uncertainty, comparison, and the silent expectation to always stay ahead. Money had become more than a tool. It had become a mental burden.

I wrote this book to explore that experience honestly.

Not from the perspective of discipline or control, but from the perspective of the human nervous system, emotional patterns, and the psychological weight money can carry in a modern, uncertain world. Calm Wealth is an invitation to step out of constant vigilance and into a steadier relationship with money, one based on clarity, self-trust, and emotional regulation rather than fear.

This is not a book about perfection. It is about sustainability. About learning how to think, decide, and live with money without letting it dominate your inner world.

If you recognize yourself somewhere in these pages, know this: nothing is wrong with you. You are not broken, irresponsible, or failing. You are responding to complexity, pressure, and uncertainty the way many thoughtful people do.

This book exists to help you respond differently, more calmly, more consciously, and more kindly.

Introduction

For many people, money is not a problem to be solved once and for all. It is a presence, sometimes quiet, sometimes loud, that follows daily life. It influences choices large and small, shapes our sense of safety, and quietly colors moments that have nothing to do with finances at all.

What makes this especially confusing is that money anxiety often appears even when things are objectively “fine.” There may be no immediate crisis, no reckless behavior, no obvious failure. And yet, the mind stays alert. Decisions feel heavier than they should. Calm feels conditional, postponed until the future is more secure, the numbers clearer, the risks smaller.

This book begins with a simple observation: money anxiety is rarely about money alone.

It is about uncertainty, responsibility, comparison, and the psychological pressure of living in a world that constantly asks us to plan, optimize, and protect ourselves against risks we cannot fully control. When money becomes the place where all of these pressures converge, even thoughtful, disciplined people can feel tense, tired, and mentally overloaded.

Most financial advice does not address this experience. It focuses on tactics, rules, and optimization, assuming that clarity comes from better information or stricter discipline. But when anxiety is involved, more information often increases pressure rather than reducing it. The problem is not a lack of knowledge. It is a lack of internal safety.

Calm Wealth takes a different approach.

Rather than asking you to control money more tightly, this book invites you to change how you relate to it. It explores the psychological and emotional forces that shape financial behavior, often more powerfully than logic or income. It examines how fear narrows thinking, how urgency hijacks decisions, and how constant vigilance slowly erodes peace of mind.

This is not a book about earning more, cutting everything back, or following rigid financial systems. It is about building a calmer, steadier relationship with money, one that supports both responsible decision-making and mental well-being.

Throughout these pages, you will learn how money anxiety develops, how to recognize your personal triggers, and how to regulate emotional responses when finances feel heavy or urgent. You will discover how to make decisions without waiting for perfect certainty, how to build systems that reduce mental load, and how to think clearly even when the future feels unclear.

The goal is not to eliminate uncertainty. That is neither realistic nor necessary. The goal is to function calmly within it.

This book is written for real life. It respects busy schedules, fluctuating income, family responsibilities, and the mental fatigue that comes from caring deeply about doing things well. It is for professionals, freelancers, parents, and anyone who feels that money occupies more mental space than it should.

You are not being asked to become fearless or perfectly confident with money. You are invited to become steadier. More aware. More grounded. Calm wealth is not about having all the answers. It is about trusting yourself enough to move forward without panic.

How to Use This Book

Each chapter builds on the previous one, moving from awareness to regulation, and from understanding to practical application. You can read the book from beginning to end, or return to specific chapters when certain financial situations feel particularly charged.

As you read, you may notice moments of recognition, discomfort, or relief. Allow them. This is not a book to rush through or "optimize." The value comes from reflection and practice, not from speed.

If at any point you feel the urge to fix everything at once, pause. Calm wealth is built gradually, through small, intentional shifts made consistently over time.

This book does not promise certainty or control. It offers something more sustainable: clarity, self-trust, and a way to live with money that does not constantly demand your attention.

If money has felt heavy, you are not alone. And you are not failing.

You are simply human in an anxious world. And learning to choose calm is one of the most valuable decisions you can make.

Chapter 1: Why Money Feels So Heavy

"Money becomes heavy the moment we ask it to provide certainty in a world that cannot."
— Ed Merid —

I once spoke with a highly capable, professional, disciplined, thoughtful, and financially responsible who admitted something quietly, almost apologetically:
"I think about money every day, even when nothing is wrong."

There was no crisis behind the confession. No debt spiral. No reckless behavior. By every external measure, things were under control. And yet, money occupied a permanent space in his mind. It followed him into quiet evenings, shaped his decisions, and subtly colored moments that had nothing to do with finances at all.

That conversation stayed with me because it revealed a truth many people struggle to articulate: money anxiety is not limited to those who are failing. It often lives with those who are trying the hardest to do things right.

When Financial Concern Becomes Emotional Overload

For many people, money rarely announces itself loudly. It shows up quietly, late at night, when the house is finally still and your mind begins to replay numbers you've already checked twice. It appears when you hesitate before clicking "confirm," even for a reasonable expense. It surfaces during moments that should feel calm, yet carry a subtle tension beneath them.

This is not panic.
It's something more persistent. More exhausting.
It's the emotional weight of money.

At first, financial concern feels practical. You plan, you calculate, you try to be responsible. But over time, concern can cross an invisible line. What was once thoughtful awareness becomes mental noise. The mind revisits the same questions again and again: *Am I doing enough? What if something goes wrong? Am I missing something important?*

Money stops being a tool and starts feeling like a constant test, one you can never quite finish.

This is where money anxiety lives. Not in dramatic crises, but in the steady pressure of always having to think ahead, always having to be careful. The heaviness doesn't come from irresponsibility. It comes from caring deeply and feeling that the stakes are high.

When money carries responsibility, identity, and future security all at once, emotional overload is not a sign of weakness. It's a predictable human response.

The Hidden Cost of Constant Money Worry

Money anxiety has a way of disguising itself as productivity. You tell yourself you're just being cautious, just staying informed. But beneath that surface, constant financial worry quietly drains mental and emotional energy.

The mind was not designed to live in a permanent state of vigilance. When money is always on your mental radar, it competes with everything else: your focus at work, your presence with loved ones, and your ability to rest. Even when you're not actively thinking about finances, part of your attention remains occupied.

This creates a background fatigue that is difficult to name but easy to feel.

Over time, this mental load changes how you experience daily life. Decisions take longer. Small choices feel heavier than they should. Conversations drift back to finances, even when you wish they wouldn't. Relationships can feel strained, not because of open conflict, but because anxiety quietly narrows emotional bandwidth.

Perhaps the most overlooked cost of money anxiety is how it erodes your sense of safety. Even when things are objectively "fine," your nervous system may remain on alert. Calm becomes conditional, something you allow yourself only after every possible risk has been accounted for.

And since no future is ever fully secure, true calm keeps getting postponed.

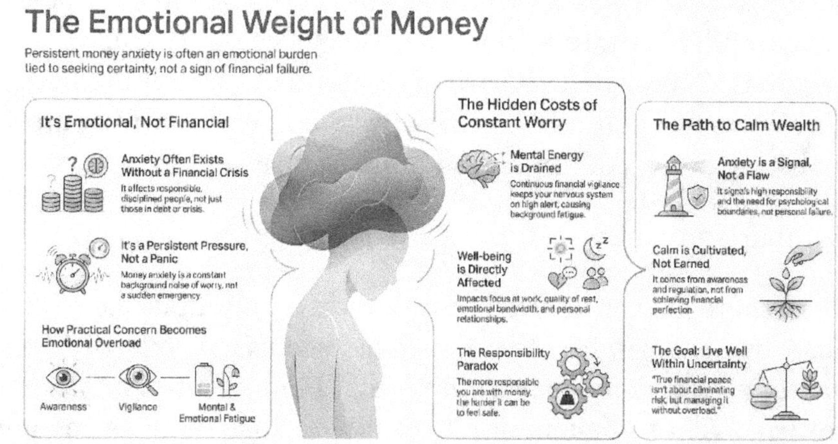

Why Responsible People Still Feel Financially Unsafe

One of the most confusing aspects of money anxiety is that it often affects the very people who are doing things right.

You plan.
You save.
You avoid unnecessary risks.
You try to be disciplined and thoughtful.

And yet, the feeling of safety remains elusive.

This paradox exists because financial anxiety is rarely about competence. It's about perception and psychology.

Responsible people tend to see further ahead. They anticipate potential problems, which is often a strength, but it can also become a source of constant pressure. When your mind is trained to look for what could go wrong, it rarely allows you to feel settled in what is currently going right.

Social comparison adds another layer. Modern life exposes us to carefully curated versions of success, stability, and progress. Even when you are making steady, sensible choices, it's easy to feel behind. There is always someone earning more, investing better, or appearing more secure.

Comparison quietly reframes adequacy as insufficiency.

Then there are the beliefs many of us carry about money, often absorbed early in life. Ideas such as *"security is fragile," "one mistake can ruin everything,"* or *"I must always stay in control."* These beliefs don't disappear just because income improves or systems are in place. Instead, they shape how safety is interpreted.

For someone operating under these internal rules, safety never feels permanent. It must be constantly defended.

Feeling financially unsafe, then, is not evidence of failure. It is typically the emotional byproduct of responsibility, awareness, and deeply ingrained beliefs about risk and control.

How Modern Life Amplifies Money Anxiety

While money anxiety has always existed, modern life has intensified it in subtle but powerful ways.

We are more informed than ever, yet rarely more at ease.

Constant access to financial information means there is always something new to worry about. News cycles highlight instability. Social platforms showcase financial milestones without context. Advice is abundant, contradictory, and often framed with urgency. The message is clear: *pay attention, or you might fall behind.*

For professionals, performance is closely tied to financial stability. Careers feel less linear, expectations continue to rise, and long-term certainty feels harder to secure.

Freelancers face a different pressure, the unpredictability of income, where calm is often postponed until the next contract, the next invoice, the next good month.

Young parents experience a shift that is both emotional and financial. Money no longer represents personal freedom alone, but responsibility for others' safety and future.

In all of these cases, the margin for perceived error feels smaller. Decisions carry more emotional weight. Even reasonable risks can feel threatening in an environment that emphasizes volatility and comparison.

Modern life doesn't just increase financial complexity; it reduces the sense of completion. There is always more to optimize, more to prepare for, more to consider.

Without clear psychological boundaries, money becomes a problem that never fully leaves the mind.

You're Not Broken, You're Overloaded

If money feels heavy, it does not mean you are bad with finances.
It does not mean you lack discipline or intelligence.

More often, it means your mind and nervous system are carrying too much responsibility without enough psychological support.

Anxiety is not a personal flaw; it is a signal. It tells you that uncertainty feels constant, that stakes feel high, and that rest has become conditional.

When money anxiety persists, the solution is rarely to try harder or think more. In fact, doing so typically increases the strain.

This chapter is not meant to offer quick fixes. Its purpose is to shift how you interpret your experience. When you understand that money anxiety is shaped by emotional patterns, cognitive load, and modern pressures, something important changes.

The self-judgment softens.
Curiosity replaces frustration.

You begin to see that calm is not something you earn through perfect behavior, but something you cultivate through awareness and regulation.

In the chapters ahead, we will explore how to work with these psychological forces rather than fight them. You'll learn how to recognize your triggers, reduce emotional reactivity, and build systems that support both financial responsibility and mental well-being.

Calm wealth is not about eliminating uncertainty.
It is about learning how to live well within it.

And for now, let this idea settle:

If money feels heavy, it's not because you're failing.
It's because you're human in an anxious world, and understanding that is the first step toward real financial calm.

Key Takeaways & Reflection

Key Takeaways

- *Money anxiety often affects responsible, thoughtful people, not those who are failing.*
- *The emotional weight of money comes from uncertainty, responsibility, and constant anticipation.*
- *Financial concern becomes exhausting when vigilance never turns off.*
- *Feeling financially unsafe is often psychological, not situational.*
- *Calm is postponed when money is expected to provide certainty in an uncertain world.*

Reflection & Practice

- *When does money feel heaviest in your daily life, quiet moments, decisions, or anticipation?*
- *What does money represent for you beyond numbers (security, control, identity, responsibility)?*
- *Notice one moment this week when money tension appears without an actual problem present.*
- *Gently remind yourself: This feeling is information, not evidence of failure.*

Chapter 2: The Mind Under Financial Pressure

"When money feels overwhelming, it is rarely because of the numbers themselves, but because of what the mind imagines they mean."
— Ed Merid —

I once worked with a freelancer whose income was stable by most objective measures. Projects were consistent. Savings existed. There was no immediate threat. Yet every time an invoice was delayed, even briefly, his entire nervous system reacted as if disaster were imminent. Sleep suffered. Concentration vanished. Decisions became rushed and defensive.

What struck me was not the financial situation itself, but the intensity of the response. The stress he felt far exceeded the reality of the risk. And once he noticed this gap, between what was happening and how it felt, something important shifted. He began to see that the pressure wasn't coming from money alone. It was coming from how his mind interpreted uncertainty.

This is where money stress truly lives.

The Psychology Behind Money Stress

Money stress rarely announces itself as a psychological issue. It disguises itself as practicality, responsibility, or foresight. You tell yourself you're just being careful, just staying informed, just planning ahead. Yet beneath these reasonable intentions, something deeper is often at work.

Financial pressure doesn't live only in spreadsheets or bank balances, it lives in the mind, shaping perception, emotion, and behavior in ways that are easy to overlook and difficult to untangle.

To understand why money feels so heavy, we must look beyond financial mechanics and into the psychology that governs how we experience risk, uncertainty, and control. Because until money stress is recognized as a mental and emotional process, it continues to operate quietly in the background, influencing decisions long before logic has a chance to intervene.

At its core, money stress is not simply about having too little or managing poorly. It is about how the brain responds to perceived threat.

Financial uncertainty activates the same systems designed to protect us from danger. When stability feels uncertain, the mind shifts into vigilance, constantly scanning for problems, anticipating losses, and preparing for worst-case scenarios.

This response is not irrational. It is human.

Money represents safety, autonomy, responsibility, and identity, often all at once. When these foundations feel unstable, the nervous system reacts accordingly. Stress hormones rise. Attention narrows. Long-term thinking becomes harder. What begins as concern slowly turns into tension, then into fatigue.

The challenge is that this response does not automatically switch off when circumstances improve. Even when income increases or systems are put in place, the mind may continue operating as if danger is imminent.

This is why money stress often persists despite "doing everything right." Without addressing the psychological layer, financial progress alone rarely brings lasting relief.

Recognizing money stress as a psychological experience, not a personal failure, is a critical shift. It moves the conversation away from self-criticism and toward understanding. And understanding is what opens the door to change.

How Fear and Uncertainty Hijack Financial Thinking

Fear has a way of shrinking perspective.

When uncertainty enters the picture, the mind prioritizes immediate safety over thoughtful strategy. In financial terms, this often leads to decisions driven more by emotion than intention.

You might recognize this pattern. A sudden expense triggers panic, even though you can technically handle it. Market fluctuations provoke impulsive moves you later question. Opportunities are avoided not because they are objectively dangerous, but because the emotional discomfort feels intolerable.

Fear doesn't just influence what you choose; it influences what you see.

Under stress, the brain favors certainty over possibility. It seeks relief, not optimal outcomes. This is why anxious financial decisions frequently feel urgent and reactive. The goal is not to make the best choice, but to reduce discomfort as quickly as possible.

For professionals, this may appear as overworking to regain a sense of control.
For freelancers, it may show up as accepting underpaid work to avoid income gaps.
For young parents, it may manifest as excessive caution or guilt around spending, even when needs are reasonable.

In each case, fear narrows the range of acceptable options, making calm decision-making feel out of reach.

Understanding this hijacking process matters because it explains why good intentions are not always enough. When fear is in charge, logic becomes a secondary voice.

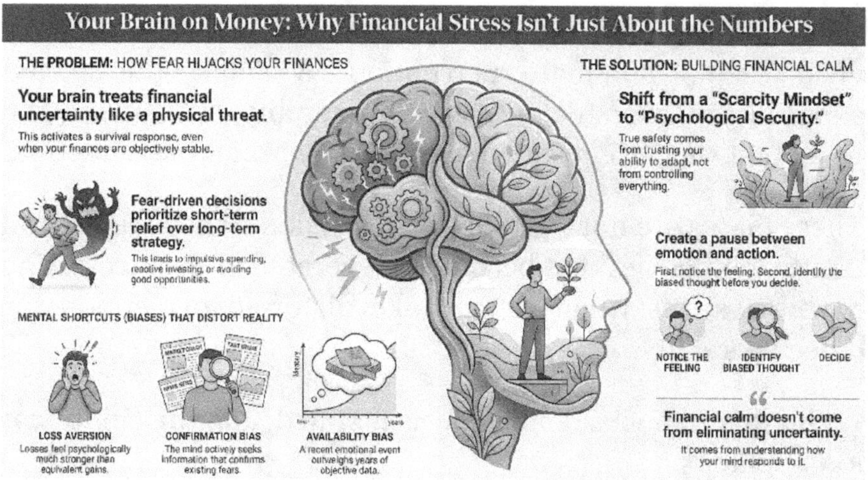

Cognitive Biases That Distort Money Decisions

Our brains rely on shortcuts, known as cognitive biases, to navigate complex situations efficiently. These shortcuts are useful, but under financial pressure, they often amplify anxiety and distort judgment.

One of the most powerful biases in money behavior is loss aversion. We feel losses more intensely than gains, which makes the possibility of losing money feel disproportionately threatening. This can lead to excessive caution, missed opportunities, or an inability to feel satisfied with progress already made.

Another common bias is confirmation bias, where we selectively notice information that supports existing fears. If you already worry about financial instability, your mind is more likely to focus on negative headlines, pessimistic opinions, or stories of failure, reinforcing the belief that danger is everywhere.

There is also availability bias, where recent or emotionally vivid events dominate perception. A single unexpected expense can overshadow years of stability, convincing the mind that such events are the norm rather than the exception.

These biases are not signs of poor judgment. They are natural mental tendencies that become exaggerated under stress. The problem arises when we mistake distorted perception for objective reality.

When that happens, anxiety feels justified, and the emotional loop tightens.

Scarcity Mindset vs. Psychological Security

A scarcity mindset is not defined by income level. It is defined by perception.

It is the belief that resources are fragile, safety is temporary, and mistakes are catastrophic. When scarcity dominates, the mind becomes preoccupied with protecting what little it believes it has, even when that belief no longer matches reality.

This mindset encourages short-term thinking. Decisions are made to avoid discomfort rather than support long-term well-being. Spending feels dangerous. Rest feels irresponsible. Planning becomes obsessive rather than supportive.

Ironically, the effort to stay safe often increases stress and reduces clarity.

Psychological security, by contrast, does not come from certainty. It comes from trust, trust in your ability to respond when challenges arise. It is the belief that uncertainty can be navigated, not eliminated.

With this mindset, money becomes a resource to manage thoughtfully, not a constant threat to defend against.

The shift from scarcity to security is subtle but powerful. It does not require ignoring risks or abandoning responsibility. It requires reframing the relationship with uncertainty, from something to fear into something to engage with calmly.

The Emotional Loop That Keeps Anxiety Alive

Money anxiety is sustained by a self-reinforcing loop.

Uncertainty triggers emotional discomfort. That discomfort leads to reactive behaviors, overthinking, avoidance, impulsive decisions, or excessive control. These behaviors may temporarily reduce anxiety, but they also prevent confidence and learning from developing.

Over time, this teaches the mind that anxiety is necessary. It becomes the signal that keeps you "safe." Calm begins to feel unfamiliar, even risky.

Breaking this loop does not start with better math or stricter discipline. It starts with awareness.

When you recognize how anxiety narrows perception, distorts judgment, and reinforces itself, you create space between emotion and action.

That space is where calm wealth begins.

A Foundation for Change

This chapter is not about fixing your finances. It is about understanding your mind under pressure.

Because until you understand how fear, bias, and scarcity shape your experience of money, every strategy will feel heavier than it needs to be.

In the chapters ahead, we will explore how to identify personal triggers, regulate emotional responses, and rebuild a sense of internal safety around financial decisions. These tools are not about becoming fearless or perfectly confident.

They are about becoming steadier, able to think clearly even when uncertainty is present.

Money does not need to control your emotional state.
But to loosen its grip, you must first understand how it took hold.

This chapter marks that turning point, the moment where money stress stops being something you fight, and becomes something you learn to work with calmly and deliberately.

Key Takeaways & Reflection

Key Takeaways

- *Money stress lives primarily in the mind, not in the numbers.*
- *Financial uncertainty activates the brain's threat-response system.*
- *Fear narrows perception and pushes decisions toward urgency or avoidance.*
- *Cognitive biases amplify anxiety under pressure.*
- *Understanding psychological patterns reduces self-judgment and restores clarity.*

Reflection & Practice

- *What financial situations trigger the strongest emotional reactions for you?*
- *Which bias do you recognize most often: loss aversion, comparison, or catastrophizing?*
- *The next time stress appears, ask: What is my mind imagining right now?*
- *Practice separating facts from interpretations.*

Chapter 3: Your Personal Money Triggers

"Until you make the unconscious conscious, it will direct your life, and you will call it fate."
— *Carl Jung* —

For years, I believed I was anxious about money because of numbers. Income. Expenses. Projections. If I could just calculate better, plan further ahead, or stay more disciplined, the tension would disappear.

But one evening proved me wrong.

I had just finished reviewing my finances. Everything was objectively fine: savings intact, bills covered, no immediate risk. And yet, as I closed my laptop, my chest felt tight. My thoughts were racing. A familiar unease settled in, uninvited and unexplained.

That was the moment I realized something important:

Money itself wasn't creating the anxiety. My internal reactions were.

That realization changed everything.

Before money anxiety can be reduced, it must be understood, not in theory, not in general terms, but in the precise moments where tension shows up in *your* life. Money triggers are not abstract ideas. They are emotional reactions that surface when a bill arrives, when income fluctuates, when someone else's success catches your attention, or when a decision feels heavier than it logically should.

Learning to recognize these triggers is one of the most powerful steps toward calm wealth.

This chapter is not about changing behavior yet. It is about awareness. Because anxiety does not appear randomly. It follows patterns. And once those patterns become visible, they lose much of their power.

Recognizing Your Money Triggers

A money trigger is any financial situation that creates a disproportionate emotional response. The situation itself may be ordinary, a routine expense, a financial conversation, a quick glance at your account, but the emotional reaction is intense or persistent.

Tightness in the chest. Irritation. Avoidance. A sudden urge to control or escape.

These reactions are not failures. They are signals.

Many people assume their financial reactions are purely logical responses to reality. In truth, money triggers are shaped by past experiences, internal beliefs, and emotional conditioning. Two people can face the same numbers and feel completely different levels of stress. The difference is not the situation; it's the meaning their mind attaches to it.

The purpose of identifying your money triggers is not to eliminate emotion. Emotion is part of being human. The goal is to recognize when emotion is driving the experience more than the facts themselves.

When you can name your triggers, you regain choice.
And choice is the foundation of calm decision-making.

Identifying Stress Patterns in Spending, Saving, and Avoiding

Money stress rarely stays internal. It shows up in patterns of behavior.

For some people, stress expresses itself as impulsive spending. Purchases are made quickly, sometimes automatically, followed by guilt or regret. The spending itself is not the real issue. It is often an attempt to regulate emotions, fatigue, frustration, or a sense of deprivation.

For others, stress appears as excessive saving or restriction. Spending feels dangerous, even when it is reasonable or necessary. Every purchase is second-guessed. Relief comes not from enjoying what money can provide, but from seeing numbers remain untouched.

Then there is avoidance, one of the most common, and least discussed responses. Bills go unopened. Accounts are checked less often. Financial conversations are postponed. Not because things are fine, but because looking feels emotionally overwhelming.

Avoidance temporarily reduces anxiety, but it allows uncertainty to grow.

None of these patterns are signs of irresponsibility.
They are coping mechanisms.

Each one serves the same purpose: protecting you from emotional discomfort. Recognizing which patterns appear in your life allows you to respond with curiosity instead of self-criticism.

Emotional Reactions Tied to Income, Bills, and Comparison

Certain financial situations are especially effective at activating anxiety because they touch deeper emotional themes.

Income changes, whether increases or decreases, often trigger identity-based reactions. A decrease may activate fear or shame. An increase can bring unexpected pressure: the fear of losing progress, of not sustaining success. Money stops being neutral and starts defining worth.

Bills, even routine ones, can carry emotional weight far beyond their actual cost. They symbolize responsibility, obligation, and time. For some, paying bills triggers resentment or exhaustion. For others, it sparks fear about the future.

Comparison is one of the most powerful money triggers of all. Seeing someone else's lifestyle, milestones, or financial success can instantly distort perception. Even when you are doing well, comparison can create the feeling of being behind. This reaction is rarely about envy; it is about fear. Fear of inadequacy. Fear of missing something essential. Fear of not measuring up to an invisible standard.

When these emotional reactions remain unconscious, they quietly shape decisions. Spending, saving, and planning begin responding to feelings rather than needs. Awareness brings these hidden influences into the open.

Media, Social Pressure, and Financial Noise

Modern life makes it difficult to separate personal financial needs from external expectations.

We are constantly exposed to financial narratives:
What success should look like.
How quickly it should happen.
What is considered "enough."

Media emphasizes extremes, rapid success, dramatic failure, constant urgency. Social platforms amplify comparison by showcasing curated moments without context. Advice is everywhere, often contradictory, and frequently framed with pressure.

The result is financial noise, information that demands attention but rarely provides clarity.

Noise increases anxiety by suggesting that there is always something else you should be doing, preparing for, or optimizing.

Part of calm wealth is learning to identify noise, and choosing not to engage with it emotionally.

A Simple Framework to Map Your Money Stressors

To transform vague anxiety into something workable, clarity is essential. This simple framework helps turn emotional overwhelm into usable information.

Step 1: Identify the Trigger
What specific situation caused this reaction?
Be precise. A bill. A comparison. A conversation. A number.

Step 2: Notice the Emotion
What did you feel, anxiety, guilt, fear, urgency, irritation?
Naming the emotion reduces its intensity.

Step 3: Observe the Behavior
Did you spend, avoid, over-control, or overthink?

Step 4: Question the Meaning
Ask: *What does this situation represent to me? What am I afraid might happen?*

Step 5: Reframe with Compassion
Instead of judging the reaction, acknowledge it:
This response makes sense given my experiences. I'm learning to respond differently.

Repeated over time, this process reveals patterns. And once patterns are visible, they become changeable.

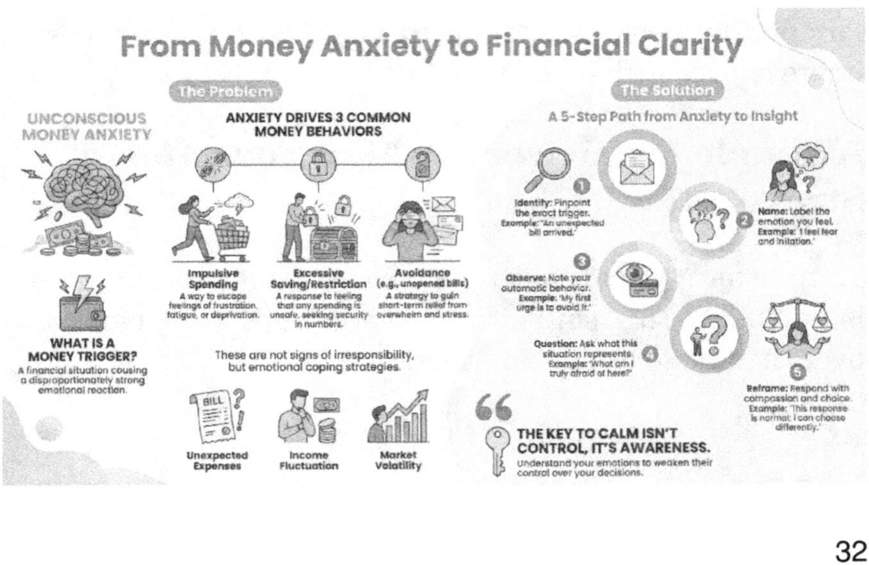

Awareness as the Turning Point

This chapter is about transforming anxiety into information. Money triggers are not enemies. They are signals pointing toward unmet emotional needs and outdated beliefs. When you listen to them without judgment, they lose their power to control your behavior.

In the chapters ahead, we will move from awareness to action, learning how to regulate emotional responses, reshape thought patterns, and build financial systems that support calm rather than stress.

But none of that is possible without first knowing what activates anxiety in the first place.

Calm wealth begins with awareness. Not perfect control. Not emotional suppression.
But understanding. And with understanding comes the freedom to choose a steadier, more intentional relationship with money.

Key Takeaways & Reflection

Key Takeaways

- *Money triggers are emotional reactions disproportionate to the situation.*
- *Stress patterns often appear as spending, over-control, or avoidance.*
- *Triggers are shaped by past experiences and beliefs, not logic alone.*
- *Awareness reduces the power of automatic reactions.*
- *Compassion creates space for change.*

Reflection & Practice

- *Identify one recurring money trigger in your life.*
- *What emotion appears first: fear, guilt, urgency, or shame?*
- *How do you usually respond, action, restriction, or avoidance?*
- *This week, practice observing the trigger without fixing it.*

Chapter 4: From Fear to Clarity

"Clarity comes not from eliminating uncertainty, but from learning how to live with it."
— Viktor E. Frankl —

There was a period in my life when I believed fear was simply part of being responsible.

I would revisit financial decisions long after they were made, running scenarios in my head, questioning choices that were already behind me. From the outside, it looked like diligence. From the inside, it felt like constant tension.

One evening, after spending hours reviewing options for a decision that did not actually require urgency, I noticed something unsettling. I wasn't seeking clarity anymore. I was trying to eliminate discomfort. Fear had quietly taken the driver's seat, convincing me that thinking more meant controlling outcomes.

That realization marked a turning point.

Fear was not protecting me. It was exhausting me.

Clarity did not arrive when I found the "perfect" answer. It arrived when I changed how I related to uncertainty itself.

Fear Thrives in Uncertainty

Fear thrives in uncertainty. It feeds on the unknown, on unanswered questions, on the belief that one wrong decision could undo everything. When it comes to money, fear often takes the lead quietly. It shapes thoughts before logic arrives, influences choices before reflection begins, and leaves many people feeling tense even when nothing is immediately wrong.

Moving from fear to clarity does not require eliminating uncertainty. It requires changing how the mind relates to it.

This chapter is about rewiring the way you think about money; not through optimism or denial, but through grounded awareness. Clarity is not the absence of risk. It is the ability to see clearly even when risk exists.

Rewiring Your Money Mindset

A money mindset is not a set of beliefs you consciously choose. It is a collection of assumptions, habits, and emotional responses built over time. These patterns were shaped by family attitudes, early experiences, cultural messages, and moments of success or failure. Once formed, they tend to operate automatically.

When fear dominates a money mindset, it often sounds like constant mental commentary:

Be careful.
Don't mess this up.
What if this goes wrong?

These thoughts may feel protective, but over time they create mental tension and decision fatigue.

Rewiring your money mindset does not mean forcing positive thoughts or ignoring reality. It means learning to question automatic reactions and replace them with responses that are more balanced and useful. The goal is not to convince yourself that everything is fine, but to create enough mental space to think clearly.

This shift begins with awareness. When you notice fear-based thoughts without immediately acting on them, you interrupt the automatic cycle. You move from reaction to reflection, and that is where clarity starts.

Separating Self-Worth from Financial Outcomes

One of the most powerful sources of money anxiety is the silent connection between self-worth and financial outcomes.

Society reinforces this link constantly. Income, status, lifestyle, and achievement are often treated as measures of personal value. Over time, many people absorb the idea that doing well financially means being worthy, while struggle or uncertainty means failure.

This belief is rarely questioned, yet it shapes emotional reactions to money in profound ways. A financial setback can feel like a personal flaw. Success can feel fragile, as if it must be constantly protected to maintain worth.

Separating self-worth from money does not mean dismissing ambition or responsibility. It means recognizing that financial outcomes are influenced by countless variables, many of which are outside personal control. Your value as a person is not determined by market conditions, income fluctuations, or temporary setbacks.

A simple exercise can help clarify this distinction:

- Write down three qualities that define your value and have nothing to do with money, integrity, creativity, care for others, resilience.
- Notice how often financial stress causes you to forget these qualities.
- Remind yourself regularly that money reflects circumstances and choices, not identity.

When self-worth is no longer on the line with every decision, the nervous system relaxes. The mind becomes more flexible. Fear loses its grip.

Replacing Panic-Driven Thoughts with Grounded Thinking

Panic-driven thoughts tend to be absolute and urgent. They frame situations in extremes:

This is a disaster.
I'll never recover.
I must fix this immediately.

These thoughts feel convincing because they are fueled by emotion rather than evidence.

Grounded thinking does not deny risk, it places it in context. It asks calmer, more constructive questions:

What is actually happening right now?
What options do I realistically have?
What is the next reasonable step?

One effective technique is the **pause-and-translate method**:

1. When a panic-driven thought appears, pause before reacting.
2. Write the thought down exactly as it appears.
3. Translate it into a grounded version.

For example:
"I can't afford this, and everything is falling apart" becomes "This expense is uncomfortable, but I can adjust and respond."

This practice reduces emotional intensity. Over time, the brain learns that panic is not the only available response.

Building Confidence Without Needing Perfect Certainty

Many people delay confidence until they feel fully prepared. They believe they must eliminate doubt before acting. In financial life, this is an impossible standard.

Confidence does not come from certainty. It comes from trust in your ability to adapt.

A growth mindset supports this form of confidence. Mistakes are not proof of failure; they are feedback. Decisions do not need to be perfect, they need to be responsive.

To strengthen this mindset:

- Focus on progress, not perfection.
- Reflect on past challenges you handled successfully, even imperfectly.

- Replace "What if I fail?" with "What will I learn if this doesn't go as planned?"

Confidence grows through experience, not prediction.

Daily Mental Shifts That Reduce Money Anxiety

Large changes come from small, consistent shifts.

Mindful Check-Ins
Once a day, notice how money feels in your body. Tension? Calm? Neutral? Observation alone reduces reactivity.

Gratitude with Precision
Focus on specific financial supports already present: a bill paid, a skill you rely on, a small buffer. Precision grounds gratitude.

Reframing Language
Replace "I can't afford this" with "This isn't a priority right now." Language shapes emotional experience.

Evening Closure
Set a boundary for financial thinking. Planning has limits. Rest is not avoidance, it is regulation.

From Fear to Clarity

Clarity is not permanent. It is a practice.

Fear may still appear, especially during change or uncertainty. But when your mindset is grounded, fear no longer controls the narrative.

You are no longer trying to silence anxiety. You are learning to interpret it.

In the next chapter, we will explore emotional regulation at a deeper level, how to help your nervous system feel safe enough to sustain calm thinking.

Because calm wealth is not built by force or perfection.

It is built one thought, one choice, and one moment of clarity at a time.

Key Takeaways & Reflection

Key Takeaways

- *Fear thrives in uncertainty, but clarity does not require certainty.*
- *Overthinking often seeks relief, not better decisions.*
- *Separating self-worth from money reduces emotional intensity.*
- *Grounded thinking replaces panic with perspective.*
- *Confidence grows through action, not prediction.*

Reflection & Practice

- *Notice one fear-based thought you frequently have about money.*
- *Translate it into a grounded version without forcing positivity.*
- *Ask yourself: What would clarity look like right now, not perfection?*
- *Practice acting on the next reasonable step.*

Chapter 5: Staying Calm When Money Feels Urgent

I still remember the email. It arrived late in the evening, subject line heavy with urgency. A financial issue that *needed* attention, now. My heart rate jumped before I finished reading the first sentence. Thoughts rushed in: *What if this goes wrong? What if I make the wrong move?* I felt the familiar pressure to act immediately, to *do something* just to quiet the discomfort.

Instead, I closed my laptop.

Not because the situation wasn't serious, but because I knew something more important than speed was at stake: clarity. Years earlier, I would have reacted from that tight, anxious place and likely made a rushed decision I'd later need to undo. This time, I paused. I regulated first. The decision came later, and it came out better.

Urgency is not the enemy. Unregulated urgency is.

This chapter is about learning how to stay calm when money feels immediate, pressing, and emotionally charged. Because the quality of your financial decisions is directly tied to the state of your nervous system when you make them.

Emotional Regulation Techniques: Why Calm Comes First

When money feels urgent, the body often reacts before the mind has a chance to engage. Heart rate increases. Breathing becomes shallow. Muscles tighten. This is not weakness; it's biology. Your nervous system is responding as if you're under threat.

In that state, your brain prioritizes short-term relief over long-term wisdom. It wants the discomfort to stop *now*. This is how people overspend, panic-sell, avoid opening bills, or agree to financial terms they later regret.

Emotional regulation is not about suppressing feelings. It's about creating enough internal stability to think clearly *with* those feelings present.

Calm does not mean passive. Calm means responsive rather than reactive.

When you regulate first, you reclaim choice.

Regulating Anxiety Before Making Financial Decisions

Urgent financial situations, unexpected expenses, time-sensitive offers, debt notices, income changes, activate fear quickly. The mistake most people make is assuming they must act *while* anxious.

A more effective approach is to check in before acting.

Ask yourself three simple questions:

1. **What am I feeling right now?** (Name it honestly: fear, pressure, shame, urgency.)
2. **Where do I feel it in my body?** (Chest, stomach, jaw, shoulders.)
3. **Is this decision truly urgent, or does it just feel urgent?**

This pause creates separation between emotion and action. It shifts you from autopilot to awareness.

Even when a decision truly is time-sensitive, regulating your emotional state first improves judgment. A regulated mind sees options an anxious mind cannot.

Remember: urgency does not cancel the need for calm; it increases it.

Practical Breathing and Grounding Techniques

You don't need long meditation sessions to regulate anxiety. You need tools that work *in the moment*. Below are techniques designed specifically for financial stress, simple, discreet, and effective.

1. The 4–6 Breath

This technique activates the parasympathetic nervous system, signaling safety to the body.

How to do it:

- Inhale through your nose for 4 seconds.
- Exhale slowly through your mouth for 6 seconds.
- Repeat for 2–3 minutes.

Longer exhales reduce physiological arousal. Use this before opening financial emails, making calls, or reviewing numbers.

2. The Feet-on-the-Floor Grounding

Anxiety pulls the mind into the future. Grounding brings it back to the present.

How to do it:

- Place both feet firmly on the floor.
- Press them gently downward.
- Notice the sensation of contact and support.
- Name silently: *I am here. I am supported.*

This stabilizes attention and reduces mental spiraling.

3. The Name-and-Orient Technique

This interrupts panic loops.

How to do it:

- Name 3 things you can see.
- Name 2 things you can hear.
- Name 1 thing you can feel physically.

It reorients the brain from threat to environment, lowering emotional intensity.

These techniques are not rituals. They are resets.

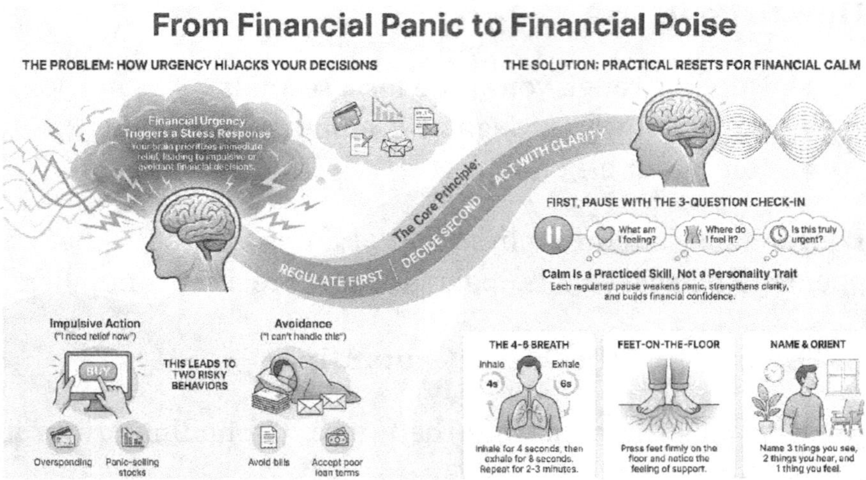

How to Pause Emotional Spending or Avoidance

Urgency often pushes behavior in two opposite directions: impulsive action or total avoidance.

Emotional spending usually says, *I need relief now.*
Avoidance frequently says, *I can't handle this.*

Both are attempts to regulate discomfort, just in different ways.

The solution is not discipline. It's pause.

The 24-Hour Rule (Modified)

For non-essential decisions made under stress, delay action for 24 hours *after regulation*, not before.

Use that time to:

- Calm your body.
- Revisit the decision with clarity.
- Ask: *Does this still feel necessary?*

The "One Small Step" Rule for Avoidance

When avoidance takes over, reduce the task until it feels manageable.

Instead of:

- "I need to fix my finances,"
  Try:
- "I'll open the document."
- "I'll look at one number."

Progress regulates anxiety. Avoidance amplifies it.

The Emotion Label

Before spending or avoiding, say:
"I am feeling ____, and I want relief."

Naming the emotion reduces its power. You may still choose to act, but now it's a conscious choice.

Training Your Nervous System for Financial Calm

Financial calm is not achieved through insight alone. It is trained at the nervous system level.

If your body has learned that money equals danger, logic alone will not override that conditioning. You must teach your system that financial engagement can be safe.

Daily Regulation Habits

- **Consistent sleep and nutrition** stabilize emotional regulation.
- **Movement**, especially walking, discharges stress hormones.
- **Short daily breathing practices** retrain baseline calm.

Predictable Money Rituals

Chaos increases anxiety. Predictability reduces it.

Examples:

- A weekly, time-limited money check-in.

- One specific place for financial tasks.
- Clear start-and-stop times for money thinking.

Structure creates safety.

Exposure with Regulation

Avoidance reinforces fear. Gentle, repeated exposure, while regulated, rewires it.

This means:

- Engaging with finances in calm states.
- Stopping before overwhelm.
- Ending with a sense of completion.

Your nervous system learns through experience, not explanation.

When Money Feels Urgent, Calm Is a Skill

Urgency will always exist in financial life. Deadlines, decisions, surprises, they're unavoidable. What *is* changeable is how your system responds to them.

Calm is not personality. It's practice.

Each time you pause instead of panic, regulate instead of react, and choose clarity over urgency, you strengthen a new internal pattern. Over time, what once felt overwhelming becomes manageable. What once triggered fear begins to trigger focus.

In the next chapter, we will explore how to create financial boundaries, mental, emotional, and practical that protect this calm and prevent urgency from constantly hijacking your attention.

Because calm wealth is not built in moments of ease.
It is built in moments that *used* to make you rush and no longer do.

Key Takeaways & Reflection

Key Takeaways

- *Urgency activates the nervous system before logic engages.*
- *Emotional regulation improves decision quality.*
- *Calm is a prerequisite for wise action, not a luxury.*
- *Small pauses prevent costly reactive behavior.*
- *The nervous system can be trained for financial calm.*

Reflection & Practice

- *Recall a recent moment when money felt urgent.*
- *How did your body respond?*
- *Practice one grounding or breathing technique before your next financial task.*
- *Remind yourself: I don't need to decide while dysregulated.*

Chapter 6: Designing a Calm Wealth System

"You do not rise to the level of your goals. You fall to the level of your systems."
— James Clear —

There was a time when my finances lived entirely in my head. Bills to remember, payments to anticipate, decisions waiting for the "right moment." I told myself I was being responsible by constantly thinking about money. In reality, I was carrying it everywhere, into conversations, into sleep, into moments that had nothing to do with finances at all.

The turning point didn't come from earning more or learning something new about investing. It came when I stopped relying on mental effort and started building systems. Quiet ones. Predictable ones. Systems that worked even when I was tired, busy, or emotionally distracted.

Calm wealth is not created by thinking harder about money. It is created by designing structures that think *for* you.

This chapter is about building a Calm Wealth System, one that reduces mental load, supports emotional stability, and fits real life.

Building a Calm Wealth Routine

A Calm Wealth System is not a complex financial machine. It is a set of simple, intentional routines that remove unnecessary decisions from your daily life.

Anxiety thrives in ambiguity. Calm grows in clarity.

When money has no structure, every financial thought feels urgent. Every expense becomes a question. Every decision demands energy. Over time, this constant low-level engagement creates emotional fatigue.

A calm system does the opposite. It creates default paths:

- Bills get paid without constant reminders.
- Savings happen without repeated decisions.
- Reviews occur at predictable times, not randomly throughout the day.

The goal is not control; it's containment.

Your finances should occupy *specific spaces* in your life, not bleed into everything else. A calm routine tells your mind, *This is handled.*

Financial Systems That Reduce Mental Load

The most effective financial systems share three core qualities: automation, simplicity, and visibility.

1. Automation: Fewer Decisions, Less Stress

Every decision you don't have to make is energy saved.

Automate:

- Recurring bills
- Savings transfers
- Minimum debt payments

Automation removes the emotional friction of "Should I do this now?" It ensures progress even on difficult days.

Automation is not loss of control; it's delegated discipline.

2. Simplicity: Fewer Categories, Clearer Thinking

Overly complex systems create confusion and avoidance.

Simplify by:

- Reducing budget categories
- Using one or two core accounts
- Choosing tools you actually enjoy using

If a system requires constant effort to maintain, it will eventually be abandoned. Calm systems are easy to return to.

3. Visibility: Calm Comes from Knowing

Avoidance often grows from uncertainty, not reality.

Create gentle visibility:

- One dashboard or app
- One weekly check-in
- One monthly overview

The goal is familiarity, not obsession. When numbers are familiar, they lose emotional charge.

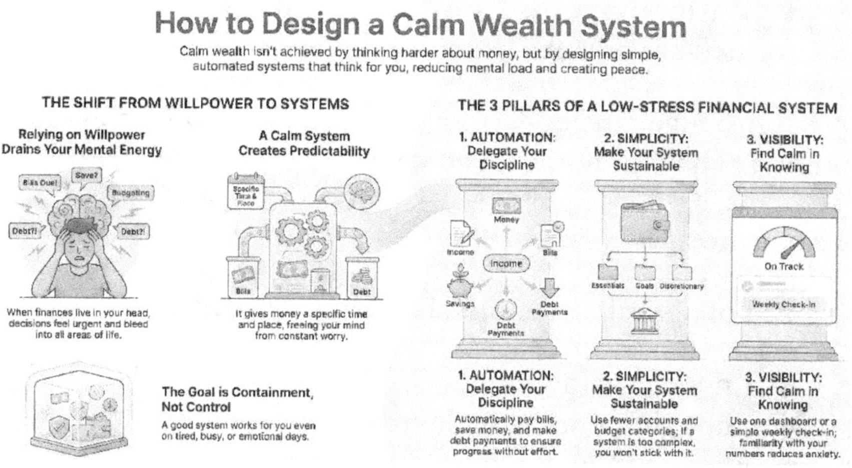

Budgeting for Peace, Not Perfection

Traditional budgeting often fails because it treats money like a math problem instead of a human experience.

A calm budget is not restrictive; it's reassuring.

Shift the Question

Instead of asking:

- *How can I control every dollar?*
  Ask:
- *How can my money support a calmer life?*

This reframing changes everything.

Principles of a Calm Budget

- **Flexibility over rigidity**: Life changes. Your budget should adapt.
- **Values before rules:** Spend intentionally where it matters most.

- **Wide margins, not tight limits**: Tight budgets increase anxiety.

A calm budget includes room for imperfection. It assumes human behavior, not ideal behavior.

The "Enough" Mindset

Instead of optimizing endlessly, define *enough*:

- Enough saving for now
- Enough spending guilt-free
- Enough tracking to feel informed

Peace comes from sufficiency, not precision.

Emergency Buffers as Psychological Safety Nets

Emergency funds are frequently discussed as financial tools. In reality, they are emotional anchors.

An emergency buffer says:
"I can handle surprises."

This belief alone reduces anxiety, sometimes more than the money itself.

Why Small Buffers Matter

You do not need a perfect emergency fund to feel safer. Even a small buffer changes your internal dialogue.

Start with:

- One month of essential expenses

- Or a fixed, comforting number

Progress builds confidence. Confidence reduces fear.

Keep It Accessible, Not Tempting

- Separate account
- Clearly labeled
- Easy to access, but difficult to spend impulsively

The purpose of this fund is not growth. It is calm.

Reframing Emergencies

An emergency fund does not eliminate stress; it shortens recovery time. Knowing you can absorb impact changes how the nervous system reacts to uncertainty.

Creating Routines That Fit Busy Lives and Families

A system that ignores real life will always fail.

Calm wealth routines must work *with* busy schedules, fluctuating energy, and family dynamics, not against them.

Time-Limited Money Rituals

- Weekly check-in: 20 minutes
- Monthly review: 45 minutes
- Annual reset: one calm session

Set a timer. When it ends, you stop. This prevents money from expanding endlessly into your mental space.

Shared Financial Language

For families or partners, calm comes from shared expectations.

This means:

- Regular, low-pressure conversations
- No ambush discussions
- Clear roles and responsibilities

Money conflict often comes from silence, not disagreement.

Gentle Defaults for Chaos Days

Plan for exhaustion:

- Automatic payments
- Pre-decided spending ranges
- Clear priorities

A calm system supports you on your worst days, not just your best ones.

From Chaos to Structure: A Personal Shift

Before I built systems, every financial task felt heavy. Even small decisions carried emotional weight because they lived in isolation. There was no container, just constant vigilance.

When I introduced routines, something unexpected happened: my mind relaxed.

I trusted the system. I stopped rehearsing scenarios. Money became something I *visited*, not something I lived inside.

That shift didn't make me perfect with money. It made me peaceful with it.

Calm Wealth Is Designed, Not Discovered

Calm is not something you wait for after everything is "figured out." It is something you build through structure.

A Calm Wealth System:

- Reduces decision fatigue
- Creates emotional safety
- Protects attention and energy

You don't need a flawless setup. You need a kind one. One that assumes stress, allows flexibility, and supports your nervous system.

In the next chapter, we'll explore how to make wise decisions when the future feels uncertain, without letting anxiety rush or freeze you.

Because true wealth is not just what you accumulate.
It's the calm you experience while managing it.

Key Takeaways & Reflection

Key Takeaways

- *Calm comes from structure, not constant thinking.*
- *Systems reduce mental load and emotional fatigue.*
- *Automation supports consistency during low-energy periods.*
- *Simplicity increases sustainability.*
- *Emergency buffers provide psychological safety, not just financial protection.*

Reflection & Practice

- *Which financial tasks currently live only in your head?*
- *Identify one small system that could replace mental effort.*
- *Where could automation reduce stress?*
- *Ask: Does my system support me on difficult days?*

Chapter 7: Making Decisions in an Uncertain World

A few years ago, I stood at a crossroads that many people will recognize. The numbers didn't line up neatly. The future felt foggy. Every option carried a mix of opportunity and risk. I waited, thinking clarity would arrive if I just analyzed a little longer.

It didn't.

What arrived instead was fatigue. The kind that comes from circling the same thoughts without moving forward. Eventually, I made a decision, not because everything was clear, but because I realized something essential: waiting for certainty had become more dangerous than choosing without it.

We live in a world where uncertainty is no longer the exception. It is the default. And learning how to make decisions calmly within that reality is one of the most important financial skills you can develop.

Decision-Making Under Uncertainty

Financial decisions used to follow a familiar script: work hard, save steadily, plan carefully, and expect relatively predictable outcomes. That script no longer fits the world we live in.

Income can fluctuate. Markets change quickly. Careers evolve. Family needs shift. Information is abundant, but clarity is rare.

Uncertainty triggers the brain's threat response. When the future feels unstable, the mind looks for safety by trying to control outcomes, or by avoiding decisions altogether. This is why uncertainty often leads to two extremes: impulsive action or total paralysis.

Neither creates calm.

The goal is not to eliminate uncertainty. That is impossible. The goal is to build decision-making skills that function *within* uncertainty, skills that allow you to move forward without panic or perfection.

Choosing Progress Over Overthinking

Overthinking feels productive. It sounds responsible. But in reality, it often serves one hidden purpose: avoiding the discomfort of action.

The mind keeps asking:

- *What if this is the wrong choice?*
- *What if I regret it?*
- *What if I wait just a bit longer?*

But most financial progress does not come from flawless decisions. It comes from *directional movement.*

The Cost of Waiting

Every delayed decision has a price:

- Missed opportunities
- Prolonged stress
- Mental energy consumed by unresolved questions

Progress creates feedback. Overthinking creates stagnation.

A Simple Shift

Replace the question:

- *What is the perfect decision?*
  With:
- *What is the next reasonable step?*

This reframing lowers pressure and restores momentum. You are no longer committing to a lifetime outcome; you are choosing a step that can be adjusted later.

Calm grows when decisions feel reversible rather than final.

How to Act Without Needing Total Clarity

Most people believe confidence comes *after* clarity. In practice, confidence often comes *from* action.

Waiting to feel certain before acting keeps you stuck. Acting thoughtfully, even while uncertain, builds trust in yourself.

The "Good Enough" Decision Framework

Ask yourself:

1. Is this decision aligned with my values?
2. Does it avoid catastrophic downside?
3. Can I adjust course if needed?

If the answer is yes, you don't need full clarity; you need commitment.

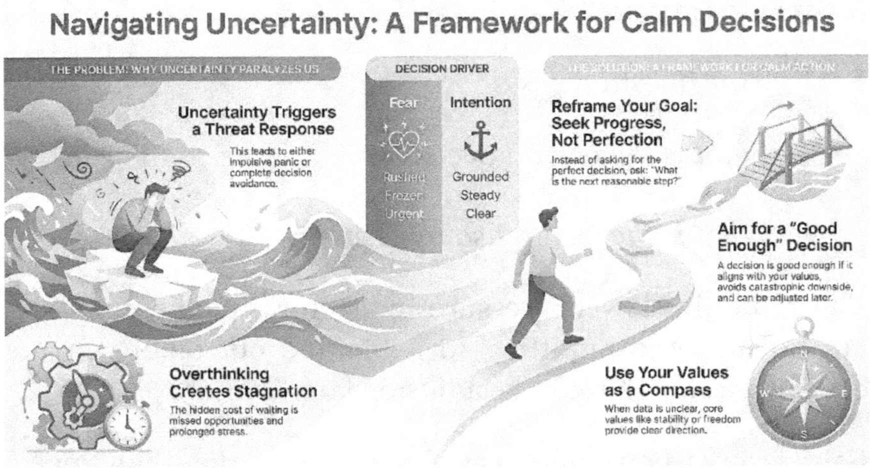

Small Bets, Not Big Leaps

Calm decision-makers rarely make all-or-nothing choices. They test, observe, and adapt.

Examples:

- Start with a smaller investment
- Try a limited change before a full shift
- Set review points instead of final judgments

This approach transforms fear into curiosity.

Emotional Check Before Action

Before deciding, pause and ask:

- *Am I choosing from fear or from intention?*

Fear-based decisions feel rushed or frozen. Intentional decisions feel grounded, even when uncomfortable.

Risk, Safety, and Long-Term Thinking

Risk is often misunderstood. It is not the presence of uncertainty; it is exposure without preparation.

True safety does not come from avoiding risk entirely. It comes from balancing risk with resilience.

Psychological Safety Matters

People make better decisions when they feel emotionally safe. This is why emergency buffers, stable routines, and clear systems matter: they create a foundation that supports thoughtful risk-taking.

Without safety, even small risks feel overwhelming.

Long-Term Thinking as a Stabilizer

Short-term fear distorts perception. Long-term thinking restores proportion.

Ask:

- *Will this matter in five years?*
- *How does this decision serve my future self?*
- *What pattern am I reinforcing?*

Long-term thinking does not guarantee success, but it reduces emotional noise.

Calm wealth is built by people who think beyond the immediate moment without disconnecting from the present.

Values-Based Decisions for Professionals and Parents

For professionals and parents, decision fatigue is real. Time is limited. Responsibility is high. This makes values-based decision-making essential.

When values are clear, decisions become simpler, even when outcomes are uncertain.

Clarifying Your Core Values

Ask yourself:

- What does financial security really mean to me?
- What am I protecting?
- What kind of life am I trying to support?

Values might include:

- Stability
- Flexibility
- Freedom
- Presence with family
- Growth

No value is superior. What matters is alignment.

Using Values as a Filter

When facing a decision, ask:

- *Which option best supports my core values right now?*

This does not remove uncertainty, but it removes inner conflict.

For parents, this might mean choosing predictability over maximum income.
For professionals, it might mean deciding sustainability over constant pressure.

Values create coherence. Coherence creates calm.

A Lesson from Uncertainty

One of the most important decisions I ever made came during a period when nothing felt stable. The data was incomplete. The advice conflicted. Waiting felt safer, but it wasn't.

I chose based on values, not forecasts. I chose a direction, not a guarantee.

That decision wasn't perfect. But it was *mine*. And that ownership created confidence that no external certainty ever could.

Uncertainty did not disappear, but my relationship with it changed.

Calm Decisions Are a Practice

Making decisions in an uncertain world is not about being fearless. It's about being grounded.

It means:

- Accepting incomplete information
- Trusting your ability to adapt
- Choosing progress over paralysis
- Letting values guide you when data falls short

You do not need to get every decision right to build calm wealth. You need to make decisions in a way that preserves clarity, energy, and self-trust.

In the final chapter, we will explore how to maintain this calm over time, how to protect it, strengthen it, and carry it forward through changing seasons of life.

Because calm wealth is not a single choice.
It is the result of many thoughtful decisions made without certainty, and without fear.

Key Takeaways & Reflection

Key Takeaways

- *Uncertainty is the default, not a temporary problem.*
- *Waiting for clarity often increases stress.*
- *Progress matters more than perfect decisions.*
- *"Good enough" decisions preserve momentum.*
- *Values-based choices reduce inner conflict.*

Reflection & Practice

- *Identify a decision you have been delaying.*
- *Ask: What is the next reasonable step, not the final answer?*
- *Which value should guide this decision right now?*
- *Notice how action changes your emotional state.*

Chapter 8: Calm Wealth for Life

There is a quiet moment I return to often. It wasn't a moment of financial success or a milestone reached. It was a moment when something unexpected went wrong, an expense I hadn't planned for, a disruption I couldn't control, and I noticed something different inside me. My body didn't tense the way it used to. My thoughts didn't spiral. I didn't rush to fix everything immediately.

I felt... steady.

That was when I understood that calm wealth is not a destination. It is a capacity. One you build over time, and one that stays with you long after specific numbers change.

This final chapter is about maintaining that capacity for years, for decades, for life.

Maintaining Long-Term Financial Calm

Financial calm is not a permanent state. It ebbs and flows with life. Careers change. Families grow. Economies shift. Unexpected events happen.

The goal, then, is not to *stay calm at all times*. The goal is to recover calm more quickly and more gently when it is disrupted.

Long-term financial calm rests on three pillars:

- Resilience: the ability to absorb impact
- Adaptability: the willingness to adjust without panic
- Self-trust: confidence in your ability to respond

When these are present, money stops feeling like a constant threat. It becomes one part of life, not the lens through which everything else is viewed.

Calm wealth is not fragile. It is flexible.

Handling Setbacks Without Emotional Collapse

Setbacks are inevitable. Missed goals. Unexpected expenses. Market downturns. Income interruptions. Even well-designed systems encounter friction.

What matters is not *whether* setbacks occur, but how you relate to them.

The Old Pattern

For many people, setbacks trigger:

- Self-blame
- Catastrophic thinking
- Emotional shutdown or frantic action

This response compounds the original problem by adding shame and urgency.

A Calmer Response

A calm response begins with normalization:

"This is part of financial life, not a personal failure."

Then comes regulation:

- Pause before reacting

- Re-anchor your nervous system
- Separate emotion from action

Finally, reflection:

- What actually happened?
- What is within my control?
- What is one constructive step forward?

Setbacks are information, not indictments. They reveal pressure points, not character flaws.

When you respond with curiosity instead of judgment, recovery becomes faster, and less painful.

Staying Grounded During Economic Uncertainty

Economic uncertainty amplifies anxiety because it feels impersonal and uncontrollable. Headlines predict danger. Numbers fluctuate. Narratives shift daily.

The mistake many people make is trying emotionally to process the entire system. That is too much for any nervous system to carry.

Calm comes from narrowing focus.

Anchor to What You Can Control

You cannot control markets, policies, or global trends. You *can* control:

- Your spending flexibility
- Your buffers
- Your decision pace

- Your information intake

This shift restores agency.

Create a Personal Financial Foundation

A calm foundation includes:

- Clear priorities
- Emergency buffers
- Predictable routines
- A long-term perspective

When this foundation is in place, external noise loses power. You may still feel concern, but not overwhelm.

Limit Financial Noise

Constant exposure to alarming information keeps the nervous system activated.

Choose:

- Specific times to check financial news
- Trusted sources
- Less frequency, more intention

Staying informed does not require staying alarmed.

Measuring Progress Without Obsession

Tracking progress is useful. Obsessing over it is exhausting.

Many people confuse awareness with vigilance. Calm wealth requires the first, not the second.

Shift from Constant Monitoring to Periodic Review

Instead of daily checking:

- Weekly or monthly reviews
- Defined start and end times
- Clear questions to answer

This prevents money from dominating mental space.

Measure What Actually Matters

Progress is not only numerical.

Also notice:

- Reduced anxiety
- Faster emotional recovery
- Improved decision confidence
- Less avoidance

These are real indicators of financial health.

Celebrate Small Wins

Calm grows when effort is acknowledged.

Celebrate:

- Consistency, not perfection
- Thoughtful decisions
- Boundaries maintained
- Emotional regulation practiced

Small wins compound into lasting peace.

Building a Lasting Sense of Financial Peace

Long-term calm is sustained through habits, not motivation.

Reinforce the Identity

Begin to see yourself as:
"Someone who handles money calmly."

Identity shapes behavior. Behavior reinforces identity.

Maintain Gentle Rituals

Regular check-ins
- Periodic resets
- Honest conversations
- Intentional pauses

These rituals signal safety to the mind and body.

Allow Evolution

What brings calm today may need adjustment tomorrow.

Life stages change. Values shift. Systems evolve.

Calm wealth allows flexibility without self-criticism.

The Quiet Achievement

Looking back, the most meaningful progress in my financial life wasn't visible from the outside. It was internal.

I stopped dreading financial decisions.
I stopped equating worth with outcomes.
I stopped carrying money anxiety into every quiet moment.

That didn't mean life became predictable. It meant *I* became steadier.

And that steadiness changed everything.

Calm Wealth Is a Lifelong Practice

This book has never been about control, certainty, or optimization. It has been about relationships.

Your relationship with money will continue to evolve. There will be calm seasons and challenging ones. What matters is that you now have tools, not just strategies, but ways of thinking and responding.

Calm wealth is:

- Making decisions without panic
- Recovering without collapse
- Progressing without obsession
- Living without constant financial tension

It is not about having enough money to stop worrying forever.

It is about trusting yourself enough to live well, no matter what the numbers are doing.

That trust is the true wealth.

Key Takeaways & Reflection

Key Takeaways

- *Calm wealth is a capacity, not a destination.*
- *Recovery matters more than permanent calm.*
- *Setbacks are information, not personal failures.*
- *Long-term calm depends on resilience, adaptability, and self-trust.*
- *Emotional peace is a valid measure of financial health.*

Reflection & Practice

- *How has your relationship with money shifted since Chapter 1?*
- *What helps you recover calm more quickly today?*
- *Which habits support long-term steadiness?*
- *Define what "enough" means for this season of your life.*

Conclusion: Choosing Calm, Again and Again

Money will never stop presenting questions.

There will always be decisions to make, uncertainty to navigate, and moments when the future feels unclear. Calm wealth was never about reaching a point where you no longer need to think about money. It was about changing how you meet those moments when they arrive.

Throughout this book, you explored why money feels heavy even when things appear stable. You learned how anxiety shapes perception, how fear narrows choices, and how modern life keeps financial pressure quietly present. You identified personal triggers, practiced emotional regulation, built systems to reduce mental load, and learned how to move forward without waiting for perfect certainty.

None of this was about eliminating risk.

It was about reclaiming steadiness.

Calm wealth is not something you achieve once and then keep forever. It is something you return to. Again and again. In small ways. A pause before reacting. A decision made from values instead of fear. A boundary that protects your attention. A system that supports you when energy is low.

Some days will feel calm. Others won't. That is not failure. That is life.

What matters is that you now understand something essential: anxiety is not a signal that you are doing something wrong. It is a signal that care, responsibility, and uncertainty are present at the same time. When you stop fighting that reality and start working with it, your relationship with money changes.

You no longer need certainty to move forward.
You no longer need perfection to feel safe.
You no longer need to carry money in every quiet moment.

Calm wealth is the ability to think clearly when things feel uncertain, to recover without collapse when setbacks occur, and to trust yourself even when outcomes are unknown.

That trust is built through practice, not prediction.

As you move forward, you will face new seasons, new challenges, and new financial decisions. When you do, return to what you've learned here. Regulate first. Think second. Decide with intention. Build systems that support you. And choose calm, not once, but repeatedly.

Not because calm guarantees success,
but because calm allows you to live well, regardless of what the numbers are doing.

That is the quiet power of calm wealth.

www.ingramcontent.com/pod-product-compliance
Lightning Source LLC
LaVergne TN
LVHW022313200926
848481LV00004B/1327
* 9 7 9 8 2 3 3 4 5 8 1 6 3 *